LIFEHACKS: 40 Tips for Rewriting Your Life

A Workbook to Help You Revitalize Your Life Mindfully

By Mira Tasich

Creative
DREAM MEDIA LLC

Creative Dream Media, llc.
Phoenix, Arizona
www.Creativedreammedia.com
www.miratasich.com

Copyright ©2017 Creative Dream Media llc.

All rights reserved. No part of this book may be used or reproduced by any means, graphic, electronic, or mechanical, including photocopying, recording, taping or by any information storage retrieval system without the written permission of the author except in the case of brief quotations embodied in critical articles and reviews.

Certain stock imagery from thinkstock.com - Images are being used for illustrative purposes only.
Cover designed by Laura Orsini – Write | Market | Design LLC

ISBN 978-0-692-87291-8
Publication date: 2017

Because of the dynamic nature of the Internet, any web addresses or links contained in this book may have changed since publication and may no longer be valid. The views expressed in this work are solely those of the author.

The author of this book does not dispense medical advice or prescribe the use of any technique as a form of treatment for physical, emotional, or medical problems without the advice of physician, either directly or indirectly. The intent of the author is only to offer information of a general nature to help you in your quest for emotional and spiritual well being. In the event you use any of the information in this book for yourself, which is your constitutional right, the author assumes no responsibility for your actions.

Be careful how you label yourself. How you feel about yourself is even more important than how others do!

-Mira Tasich

Table of Contents

Introduction 1

How to Use This Workbook 6

Emotional Repair 10

PART I: Dealing Directly with the Initial Impact 13

    What NEWS BREAK Did You Receive? 13

    TIP #1 – Believe It; Don't Deny It! 15

    TIP #2 – Don't Panic! Remain Calm 17

    TIP #3 – Deal with the Sadness 21

    TIP #4 – Deal with the Anger 25

PART II: Holistic Self-Care 28

    TIP #5 – Detox 31

    TIP #6 – Massage Therapy 34

    TIP #7 – Recuperate/Heal 36

    TIP #8 – Commit to Hiatus or Take a Short Pause 39

    TIP #9 – Explore Nature's Hot Springs 41

    TIP #10 – Get a Makeover/Pamper Yourself 44

    TIP #11 – Dance 49

    TIP #12 – Spiritual Renewal 51

    TIP #13 – Create Your Own Zen-like Space or Experience ... 53

TIP #14 – Music Therapy 57

PART III: Re-Channeling of Energies 61

TIP #15 – Get to Know the Real You 62

TIP #16 – Keep a Journal 65

TIP #17 – Travel or Act as a Tourist in Your City 68

TIP #18 – Find a Hobby 71

TIP #19 – Expand Your World – Keep on Learning 73

TIP #20 – Get Your Creativity Flowing 76

TIP #21 – Volunteer 81

TIP #22 – Spread Kindness 85

TIP #23 – Expand Your Vision 89

TIP # 24 – Passion Meets You 93

Part IV: Life & Career Rejuvenation 96

TIP #25. Redefine/Reinvent Your Purpose 98

TIP #26 – Develop Your Plan of Action 101

TIP #27 – Go into Action 106

TIP #28 – Socialize/Network/Search for Support 108

TIP #29 – Look the Part 111

V. Stay in the CEO Lane of Your Life 114

TIP #30 – Living with the "New Normal" 118

TIP #31 – Stay Positive 123

TIP #32 – Be Flexible 127

TIP #33 – Create Your Own Uplifting Drill 130

TIP #34 – Build Your Inspirational Boost File 133

TIP #35 – Embrace Diversity (Yours and Others) 136

TIP #36 – Retool Your Attitude Continuously 139

TIP #37 – Realign Your Actions to Retain Balance 141

TIP #38 – Reflect (Ongoing) 145

TIP #39 – Think "Proactively" 148

TIP #40 – Love Yourself, Always 150

Conclusion 154

Planning & Progress Tracking 157

Activity Sheet 158

ABOUT THE AUTHOR 162

Introduction

Are you feeling defeated, powerless, or frustrated with your current position in the human race? What is bothering you?

>Career?
>
>Finances?
>
>Relationship?
>
>Life in general?
>
>All of the above?

Are you facing a problem but have no clue how to resolve it? Do you just wish things were different? Or, do you specifically hope for the perfect idea that will make you a successful entrepreneur? Are you ready to change your career?

Perhaps you've been laid off from your job or have experienced a significant change affecting your current job status. Or, maybe you got fed up with your current career and want to experiment with a different one, or even start a new chapter in your life after retiring. What are you going to do? What should your next move be? You can update your résumé – and perhaps wonder why you haven't been doing this all along – call some contacts, and talk to friends and family who might have ideas.

But what will significantly propel you to the next phase of your life?

Every individual's reaction to an unexpected event varies. You might be angry and fired up. You may experience anxiety or high stress and worry that you don't have any options. Surprisingly, you may initially feel relief until the depression and hopelessness start to set in.

Whatever obstacle you are facing, **YOU** hold the answers to reconciling your dilemma. **No one else does.** You are responsible for your thoughts and actions. The point is that you still need to create a personal plan and discover the will to achieve your desired outcome. You may blame other people or situations for your misery or lack of motivation, and perhaps you may have the right to. Remember, however, that you alone can control these thoughts. And, you'll need to control them if you are to move forward in any meaningful way. So, to quote Cher's character in *Moonstruck*, "Snap out of it!" Get over whatever is causing you to stay in limbo and start implementing steps toward your reinvention. Clearly, this is your chance to re-write your story.

Are you ready to open this gift that's been handed to you, albeit unexpectedly?

Don't ever fall into the trap of despair and decide – consciously or unconsciously – to stay there. You cannot accomplish anything by labeling yourself a victim and you won't get rid of your issues by attempting to mask them with alcohol or drugs. Instead of complaining and organizing a pity party, cancel the invitations you were planning to send to your walking zombie pals and retool your attitude.

No matter what happens in life, seek serenity and keep reinventing yourself until you are truly happy. If you unclutter your mind and fill it with appreciation and love instead of focusing on the negative, good things are sure to come your way. Modern life doesn't always make this easy. We're plugged in and turned on all day and all night. Yes, despite the advantages technology provides us, our intuition, creativity, and wisdom are still necessary to live life fully. If technology consumes our days and our nights, we face the danger of losing our spiritual connection – and our connection to one another. Blocking our inner voice – our authentic self – is not a good idea. And, it's a poor substitute for real relationships. To make decisions in our best interest, we need to stay true to ourselves.

Would you be willing to turn off your phone for an hour every day if you knew doing so would help you create the life of your dreams?

How do you know where to start? Based on my personal journey of reinvention, years of experience, and the subsequent wisdom I have gained, I have created a step-by-step program to help you proceed into your next phase in life.

As I wrote my book, **Good Bye Job, Hello Life**, I learned the importance of seeking solitude and listening to my inner wisdom. Both activities lifted me after I lost my long-term career. I realized I had subconsciously used these techniques in the past when faced with challenges. The job loss taught me to recognize and appreciate these easily accessible tools. In addition, remaining open minded, staying on track, and nurturing my creativity guided me. A higher power had made a plan and led me into discoveries I did not even understand at the time. This serendipitous process freaked me out a little. Though I was silently despondent, the Universe was lining up the people, the events, and the actions I needed to discover and take. I was persistent, regardless of interruptions and other obligations. If you are patient, open-minded, and true to your heart, you will get there, too.

Decide to BE in the CEO LANE of Your Life!

As most of you know, a CEO of an organization is the Chief Executive Officer. Immediately, you **VISUALIZE** someone with money, status, and power – a person who makes the company's final decisions. The best CEOs are smart, capable, well-spoken, and inspirational to others because of their visions and beliefs. They have their acts together. All their shareholders and employees expect them to know what is best for the organization as they make decisions. They possess strategic thinking skills, communication skills, and leadership skills – all necessary for taking their companies to new heights of success. While not all **CEOs are** smart, capable, or inspirational, just the term *CEO* makes us think of someone powerful and in control. We often forget that **we are the CEOs, the shareholders, and the employees of our own destinies,** so we need to model the best attributes of CEOs and apply them to every aspect of our lives. If we act as the CEO of our **lives**, we know how to direct our healing, drive our success, and implement strategies for our happiest outcomes.

Are you ready to re-write your life?

How to Use This Workbook

You are in control, and this may be the first time you have had the opportunity to take actions on your own, instead of being told what to do by someone else (e.g., a parent, teacher, minister, scout leader, boss, supervisor, or partner). It's not important where you start; it's more important **that you start**.

Step 1 – Read through each segment. How much time you devote on each segment is totally up to you.

- ☐ Pick up a notebook or journal to record your answers.
- ☐ The Segment Table and Activity Sheet forms are available for you to track your progress. You may download them at **miratasich.com**.

Step 2 – Determine which segment you want to focus on first. For greater success, however, I recommend that you follow the plan in sequential order.

- ☐ Be honest with yourself.
- ☐ Listen to your heart.

Step 3 – Arrange the rest of the segments so that you have an initial action plan that makes sense for you.

- ☐ Don't stress too much over the order of the segments; you can always adjust the order later.
- ☐ Pick up crayons and take a coloring break.
- ☐ Enjoy the ride!

Mira Tasich

You are now officially moving into the

CEO lane of your life!

Emotional Repair

Your emotional state of mind will dictate your success, and it needs to be examined – and perhaps adjusted – before you begin any project. Regardless of the situation you are in, if you approach it from a positive, calm, reasonable, mindful perspective, you have a better chance at resolving your obstacle, adapting to change, or overcoming the odds you are facing. I highly recommend working out your frustrations; wiping out negativity, blame, and anger and ridding yourself of any other real or imagined block helps you take a positive first step. **You need to start with a fresh attitude.**

In this segment I have given you tools that worked for me. Experiment and determine what works for you. Repeat the process as many times as you need to – and do not move on to realizing your passion, new partner, or career interest until you are emotionally ready to do so.

.

Mira Tasich

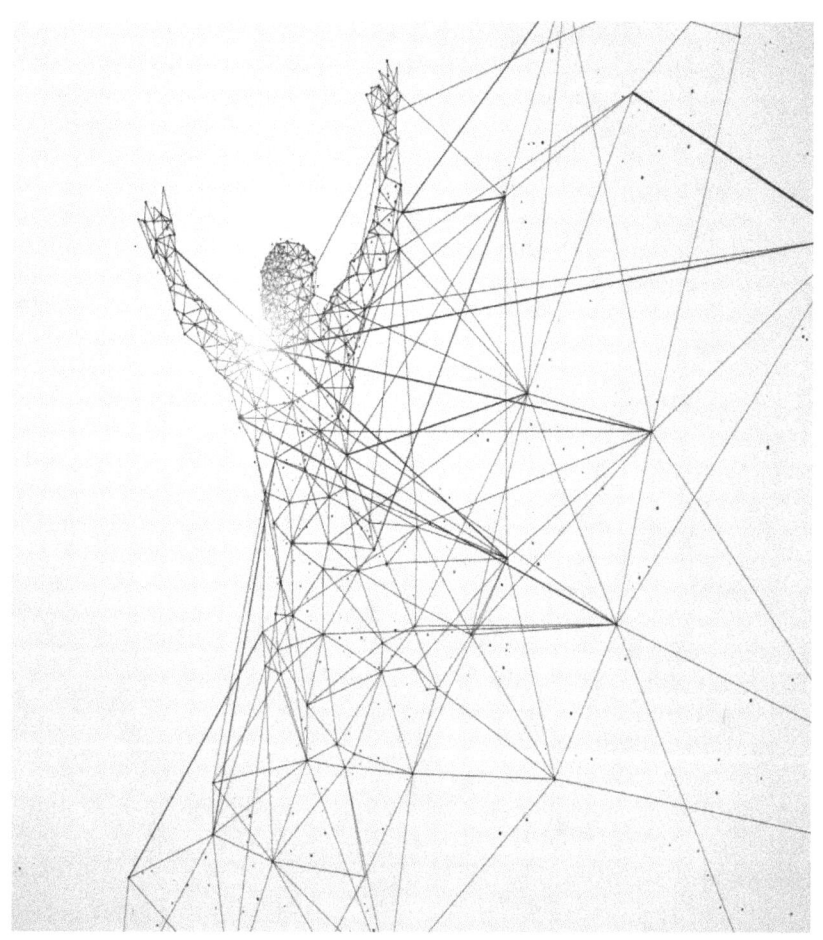

Wipe out negativity, blame, and anger.

LIFEHACKS: 40 Tips for Rewriting Your Life

PART I: Dealing Directly with the Initial Impact

What NEWS BREAK Did You Receive?

A personal announcement was delivered to you, telling you of an unexpected change. You received a pink slip for the job you really were not all that excited about, but the money paid bills. Your spouse of twenty years asked for a divorce, leaving a marriage that had lost its spark ten years ago. Financial struggles are causing you to leave a home you love. Or, you became an empty nester, struggling with this new void and a lack of purpose. Whatever the change is – it's a big one – and you're going to have to deal with it.

Losing any type of a job, for whatever reason, is difficult. Being rejected by the company where you worked hard to earn praise, credibility, importance, and merit – not to mention your pay and benefits – is life altering. Yet, layoffs and suggested early retirements are common occurrences these days. Today's workers don't have the security nets offered in the past. Corporate downsizing is almost expected in many industries and it is understandable. Corporations will do whatever they need to do to survive, taking steps they feel are necessary to remain financially healthy. Perhaps you didn't lose your job, but you got angry with your manager and impulsively quit without obtaining a new one first.

Even if the change is something other than a job loss, you have been thrown out of your comfort zone. Losing a marriage – or a loved one – is devastating. And depending on your resilience, recovery might be a long way off.

Perhaps you haven't received any life changing announcement, but for one reason or another you feel as if you have lost your energy or inspiration or humor, and you really need a change. Even if you are simply unhappy with your life or current career, you might be ready to rewrite your story.

What is your news break? Say it, write it down, and shout it to the world, even if you are alone inside your house.

TIP #1 – Believe It; Don't Deny It!

Many twelve-steppers are familiar with the phrase, "Denial is not a river in Egypt." It's true – denying reality isn't going to help you deal with it. So let the news soak in and realize that you are not alone. Disappointing events happen to all of us – it's a part of life. Although the news may be life-altering, it is not the first obstacle you've had to overcome. And guess what – you overcame those past obstacles. Regardless of what it was, you got up and got over it. Overcoming obstacles is not only a part of life, but it also enriches our character.

QUESTION 1: How can this news work for you instead of against you?

QUESTION 2: How can you turn this negative moment into a positive?

QUESTION 3: What opportunity does this sudden change provide that could not have happened otherwise?

QUESTION 4: What can you do to shift your perspective? How about watching something funny? Definitely rest and have a treat.

LIFEHACKS: 40 Tips for Rewriting Your Life

Get up and get over it…..

TIP #2 – Don't Panic! Remain Calm

It is, unfortunately, human nature to worry. Our thoughts often immediately land on the negative side of the equation. If someone dumped you, you may find yourself thinking, *I will never meet anyone else again.* But you will. People do all the time. Their lives go on. When we lose our jobs, we have a tendency to automatically think, *I am going to lose my home, my car, and my possessions. I will never find another job. I am too old for anyone to hire me. I am too inexperienced or too young to get the job I really want.*

Stop the panic! Stop the blame! Stop listing the negatives that might happen!

Refuse to entertain any negative thoughts. Instead, do some breathing exercises. Disconnect your imaginary panic button and throw it into the trash. If you find yourself jobless, do not rush or feel obligated to make any big career decisions immediately. However, depending on your finances, you might have to obtain a short-term paying position for income and strive to land the one you love a bit later. If your newsbreak was not career related – or you don't need to work, but you need a life makeover – you may be in a more favorable position, at least as far as work goes. Your life makeover will be likely easier if you don't have to worry about your immediate finances.

QUESTION 1: What do you typically do when you panic about something? More importantly, does it help resolve the panic and restore equilibrium? Or, does it serve to send you down a path of negativity that is hard to come back from?

QUESTION 2: What are you afraid of? What is the worst that could happen? How likely is it to really happen? What would you do if it did?

QUESTION 3: Now, reframe those thoughts. How can you turn your obstacle into a positive force for you? What would you do if panicking weren't an option? You, alone, are in charge of giving your setback a positive spin.

Disconnect your imaginary panic button and throw it into the trash.

TIP #3 – Deal with the Sadness

Recognize that your emotions are valid. If you feel like crying, let yourself cry. Get it all out. But then, shake it off.

We all deal with disappointments differently. For many of us, a trusted friend or confidante we can talk to candidly will help. Somehow just verbalizing the problem and discussing it helps us get it out of our system. Holding on to negative thoughts impedes your ability to clean your slate and start fresh.

Perhaps you just need to change your **perspective** – get out of your physical space because it might be keeping you stuck in a negative emotional state. Have a delicious lunch, take a nap, or see a funny movie. One therapeutic exercise encourages you to go to a Zen setting, preferably outdoors - weather allowing, and asks you to people watch. Everyone has a story and it is diverting to guess a person's story. Perhaps it is similar to your story. Are they at the Japanese Botanical Garden at 11 a.m. on a workday because they got laid off, too? Use your imagination.

The key is to get over the initial wave of disappointment quickly. For some, it might take a few hours and for others a couple of days or longer. Put every effort into making sure it doesn't go beyond a couple of days.

QUESTION 1: What was your initial reaction to the shocking news or event you experienced?

QUESTION 2: Now that you've had a bit of time to process the information, how are you responding? Is your reaction more positive and hopeful or more negative and focused on the adversity of your situation? You will likely find yourself vacillating between the two – but what is your default reaction? Where do you spend the most time?

QUESTION 3: If you're in a more negative thought pattern about your unexpected life change, what are ten things you could do today to shift into a more positive focus? Big or small, silly or serious – just write them down. Don't let cost, feasibility, or appropriateness factor into your list. Now, pick one and go do it!

Mira Tasich

The key is to get over the initial wave of disappointment quickly.

TIP #4 – Deal with the Anger

An undesirable event happened, and it was caused by something or someone. In your eyes, what are the sources of your problems? If you are angry about your newfound situation – and you may have every right to be, you might be focused on blaming certain people. You feel like telling them a million things – so start a fresh page in your journal and write them all down. All of them. Turn your anger into words and get them all out of your head. Just put the **angry words** on paper. You don't have to share these thoughts with anyone – this is **FOR YOUR EYES ONLY!**

Once you are done, hit the **"DELETE"** button to erase the list or letter or note from your computer – and your mind. If you handwrote your note, do something to destroy it. Shred it, turn it into a paper airplane you sail into your recycle bin, or use it as a mat to perform a tap dance.

One of the worst things you can do to sabotage your well being and future success is to internalize the anger, turning yourself into a victim.

Getting rid of the anger is the first step toward your self-care – and moving into an attitude where you can begin to see the gift in this unforeseen life challenge. Forgiving people is crucial. Not doing so makes it more difficult to have a peaceful life and a clear mind. Spend your focus and energy on future not on your past.

QUESTION 1: Why are you angry? Yes, this might seem obvious, but write out the answer anyway.

QUESTION 2: To whom is your anger directed? When you take a moment to think about it realistically, is this the person who deserves the blame? Did she or he alone – without input from any other person on the planet – cause your present situation?

QUESTION 3: OK – this may be a hard one, but I know you can work through it! How much did your own thoughts, attitude, behaviors, or beliefs have to do with creating the situation you are in? Walk away from the question for a few minutes to think, but be as truthful as you can possibly be when you answer this question.

QUESTION 4: How much of your anger is directed at yourself?

What can you do right now to begin releasing that anger and moving toward forgiveness and joy? Start by writing down in your journal a letter of forgiveness (even if it's only to yourself).

Just put the **angry words** on paper. You don't have to share these thoughts with anyone – this is **FOR YOUR EYES ONLY!**

PART II: Holistic Self-Care

Now is the time to start the healing process – spiritually, physically and emotionally. The definition of holistic health care is: **"treatments of the whole person: mind, body and spirit."** Recently the medical industry began realizing the importance of a holistic approach to healing. It makes sense that we embrace all of the aspects of our being.

I must admit this is not always easy. While I have perfected some areas of self-care, I still struggle with eating a healthy diet daily. In spite of focusing on eating more veggies, I still have weaknesses for chocolate, bacon, and cheese, and they're tough to resist. In addition, Euro Bakery, located near me, makes a wide range of out-of-this-world cookies and cakes. They sell their delicious homemade cakes by the slice, and it is, at times, impossible to drive by and not stop for a treat. On the other hand, for the last couple of years, I have been using Juice Plus+ supplements, shakes, and nutritional bars, plus an Omega 3 supplement to help balance my meals. My family doctor encouraged me to drink a glass of green juice daily and when I don't have time to make it at home, I visit a place I recently discovered: O2 Juice Bar & Spa. Since I do try to avoid sugar, my favorite treat there is Liquid Life (made of all green vegetables). I have learned that we are actually what we eat, so I am trying to align my diet with my vision of what I truly am. We cannot neglect our nutritional and psychological "self." It is a lifestyle change, and while I dropped a number of bad habits, I still have few to eliminate. The key is not to give up.

Thankfully, I believe I have mastered reflecting and building up my emotional and spiritual resilience when something upsets me. I learned through my experiences and journey of recovery after my job loss. In my Chapter 27 of my book, **Good Bye Job, Hello Life**, "Finding A Way," I wrote: *"I went through various steps of self-discovery including quieting my mind, reflecting, re-connecting spiritually, opening my senses to embrace my authentic self and going crazy with creativity. Experimenting with artistic endeavors helped me restore balance and create harmony and happiness. Once I uncovered the project I wanted to pursue as a potential career, I attempted to create a vision of it."* At the time, I did not realize what I had discovered, nor its importance to my rejuvenation. But I now recognize its magnitude.

These are some tools you can experiment with, but you will find your own personal way of self-care, depending on what your priorities are.

Embrace all of the aspects of your being.

TIP #5 – Detox

The best way to kick off a holistic self-care process is to do a cell detox, starting with a tub soak. Tense muscles and stress evaporate with a soothing bath. Fill your tub with warm water and add any variety of bubble bath, Epsom salt, or detox powder (find three recipes here: **wellnessmama.com/8331/detox-bath-recipes**). Relax for 15 to 20 minutes. If you would like, light some scented candles, but be careful not to start a fire! Perhaps you would enjoy some soft music in the background – or maybe you just prefer a quiet environment.

Close your eyes and allow yourself to release any thoughts that might worry you. Imagine all the bad energy exiting your body. Then refocus and enjoy the scent and warmth of the water. Be in the present. It might help to choose a single word to focus on: love, joy, happiness, success, fulfillment, presence, bliss, health, wonder. Choose a word that resonates with you. Then, when the negative thoughts try to intrude, go back to your word and send those thoughts packing. Imagine yourself enjoying a favorite vacation spot, a delightful memory from your past, or the wonderful future you would like to create.

A tub soak is just one way to relax, but they're not for everyone. What are other ways you can relax, unwind, release worries and simply reconnect? If you do not have a tub, take a steamy detox shower. Soak a rag or sponge with your favorite body wash and as you apply it and rinse it off, imagine all the toxins leaving your body. Then wrap yourself in a towel or robe and sit comfortably thinking about something fun, as mentioned above.

For additional pampering, apply a body lotion or one of your favorite pure essential oils.

QUESTION 1: The word *detox* means to remove toxins. Toxins can be physical things, like poison or venom, but they can also be negative thoughts. What are a few toxins you would like to release from your body – or your life?

QUESTION 2: If you chose a word to focus on, what is that word? How can you use that word in your life to help motivate you and keep your thoughts positive?

QUESTION 3: Did you ever try one of the juices at the o2 Juice Bar and Spa? My favorite is Liquid Life, a green drink without sugar (organic cold pressed juice). For an ultimate detox process, you might want to try one of the many options that various places offer. Or you can make it at home. It is a perfect way to promote health inside and out. Of course, check with your doctor first (especially if you plan to do it for a longer period of time).

Imagine all the bad energy exiting your body...

TIP #6 – Massage Therapy

Many people do not realize the benefits of massage therapy, but it is one of the easiest ways to reset your spiritual and physical state. If you feel stressed, do the bath detox first, and then go for a massage immediately afterwards. There are many kinds of massage, so do some research to find out which one might be most beneficial to you. According to the Mayo Clinic, massage therapy can help a person reduce anxiety and relieve headaches. You can read about the many benefits of massage therapy here: **arealrelief.massagetherapy.com/benefits-of-massage**.

If you think you can't afford this treat, find a local massage school, look for a special, or offer to trade massages with your spouse or a friend.

QUESTION 1: In our harried, plugged-in, always-on-the-go world, we often ignore the power of human touch. A massage can go a long way towards allowing you to reconnect and feel your body again. How do you feel about physical contact with others? Does it depend on who the person is and how well you know them?

QUESTION 2: Hugs are another great way to connect with each other. It's said that every person should get at least 12 hugs a day. How many hugs do you give and receive daily? If it's on the low side, what can you do to begin inviting more hugs into your life? (Pssssttt: They're a lot less expensive than massages!)

TIP #7 – Recuperate/Heal

We tend to think of recuperation and healing as something reserved for those who've had illnesses or injuries. But the fact is that most of us are not treating our bodies with the reverence they deserve. Just about every one of us is guilty of not getting enough sleep. Many of us eat food that's not good for us because fast food is quicker, easier, and cheaper. We are addicted to sugar. We drink too much and exercise too little. Better diets, more exercise, more sleep and more massages can jump start recuperation and healing. Nurturing your body produces instant results. Do what you can to avoid the chemicals. Remember, escaping your pain with drugs and alcohol is a short-term fix that may leave you in even worse shape later. Reduce your sugar intake. Reach for a cup of green tea. Start reading food labels and researching ingredients. It is OK to take baby steps. If you have a setback, do not get angry at yourself and do not give up.

As mentioned in the introduction, you are responsible for your thoughts and actions. Emotional healing is a large part of your recuperation. We are all influenced by our cultural backgrounds, our families and the psychological barriers formed by our personal history. If you decide to leave a bad relationship or a miserable job, do not feel guilty after you make your decision. Instead, congratulate yourself for the courage to make the change and move forward without regrets.

QUESTION 1: How well do you take care of your physical body?

QUESTION 2: If you've been neglecting your body lately – carrying some extra weight, ignoring a particular ache or pain, smoking or drinking to excess – what is one thing you can do today to begin taking better care of your body so that it can help you achieve your dreams and carry you through to your next chapter in life?

QUESTION 3: How can you celebrate that first step you took into a positive habit that helps your body become stronger and more vibrant?

Question 4: What can you do to control your thoughts and actions? Make sure you have written down your personal power boosts and then read them when you start feeling guilty.

TIP #8 – Commit to Hiatus or Take a Short Pause

According to the American Academy of Pediatrics, *"Recess is a necessary break in the day for optimizing a child's social, emotional, physical, and cognitive development."* If we know it's important for kids to take breaks, why do we seem to forget this as we grow into adulthood? Committing to taking regular time out should be easy, right? Wrong. Many people cannot do this properly, if at all. Years ago when I visited my uncle in Lyon, France, I was amazed when everything shut down at noon and people took naps. I was encouraged to do the same.

One of the best ways to tap into your intuition and creativity is by embracing recess based on your personal time allotment. Taking time out is a particularly good idea if you find yourself feeling confused and depressed. For the electronically obsessive individual, watching a fun or educational TV show may be your easiest choice. However, reading an inspirational book, taking a walk, or sitting outside will likely be more beneficial. Just take enough time to improve your mindset. Even a short 20- to 30-minute nap can help.

For corporate employees, a nap may not be a possibility; however, you may be able to use your lunch hour to put your head down for few minutes or perhaps, weather allowing, a short rest in the car.

QUESTION 1: How often do you pause during the day, if even for a moment? If your answer is "Never," you need to begin taking some time out periodically throughout your day to pause and reconnect with yourself.

QUESTION 2: What can you do to remind yourself to take a pause during the day? One great idea is to attach it to something you already do regularly. Take two minutes to step outside after each meal. Google "one-minute meditation" and find one that works for you – and then practice it each time you go to the bathroom throughout the day. Take an extra minute or two before getting out of your car every time you arrive at a destination to center yourself.

TIP #9 – Explore Nature's Hot Springs

If you live close to natural hot springs, they are an ideal way to relax and rejuvenate. Be brave and try something new. For example, Glen Ivy Hot Springs in Corona, California (**glenivy.com**), offers a number of indulging pools, seating areas in lush landscapes, and various wellness treats for those wanting head-to-toe spa pampering. The treatments can be purchased individually or in packages. But a more frugal way would be to purchase an all-day pass (Taking the Waters admission M-F offer cheaper options) so that you can enjoy the pools on your own or have lunch at their café. You can sit in a hot spring full of natural minerals, cover your body with mud that leaves your skin as soft as a baby's face, or swim in a salt pool, hot or cold. All you need is a bathing suit and money for lunch or their gift shop – towels, body wash, and shampoo are provided by the spa. They also offer various workshops and mindful fitness classes.

I remember the first time my husband and I went to Glen Ivy Hot Springs. As we entered the Spa, the landscaping – the strategically placed flower beds and pots and the little fountains – relaxed me before I had even entered the hot springs. Walking throughout the complex, I felt connected to nature, admiring the plants I normally do not see in Arizona, and I knew this was definitely a place to find tranquility and rejuvenation. I had one problem. Since I left my purse and camera in the locker, I could not take any pictures while I admired the pretty settings. When I was covered in mud, I asked one lady to take a shot and email it to me, but I never received the photo. Since my husband and I grew in Europe, visiting hot springs was something very familiar to us. Europeans believe in the health benefits of hot springs. Whether that is truth or fiction, I don't know, but one thing I do know – sitting in natural mineral-rich hot water not only soothes and relaxes, but it also feels like a healing agent. There is something very therapeutic and beneficial about soaking in a natural hot springs. My husband and I left very refreshed and re-energized. To me this was a perfect Zen place to rejuvenate and relax.

Here is a list/map of hot springs in the United States: **acme.com/jef/hotsprings**. Based on an initial glance at the map, chances are good there's one within driving distance of you. Here is a link to a list of hot springs around the world, by country: https://en.wikipedia.org/wiki/List_of_hot_springs.

QUESTION 1: How often do you allow yourself to just get away from it all? Do you have a favorite place or one you've been meaning to visit? Now that you have the time, what's keeping you from getting in the car or catching a bargain flight and just going? There are always ways to conserve money – try not to let the cost always be your reason for not doing something.

QUESTION 2: What type of natural setting would most inspire you?

Time out is great, especially in nature. Sit by the window, outside, or decorate your work area with plants (if allowed), and photos of beautiful scenery.

TIP #10 – Get a Makeover/Pamper Yourself

Continue to focus on uncovering and nurturing yourself.
You are special. Do you love yourself? Do you understand your own needs and wants? Chances are you were last on your list of priorities for much of your life. Now it is time to really focus on yourself. It is all about loving yourself enough to explore some pampering that will leave you feeling special.

Get a facial, manicure, pedicure – all of them if you can afford it. These days, you can find coupons from sites like Groupon or Living Social, making these services much more affordable. Get a haircut or color change. Okay, if that is too drastic for you, perhaps just style it a bit differently. If money is tight, try to locate a local cosmetology school; their students can glorify you with a new look for a much smaller price. Whatever other makeovers you might undertake is completely up to you. A new look or fun treat can boost your confidence and help you embrace your New Life Transition process.

I remember when I was laid off, I'd heard about a new salon located less than five miles from my home in Michigan. Hollywood stylist, Ken, had opened this elegant hair salon; at the time, he was doing Jessica Simpson's hair, Celine Dion's, and many cover models' hair. I made an appointment and received a consultation, and later a haircut, from Ken. I told him to say hello to one of my favorite singers at the time, Celine. I was so excited to receive this star treatment and it immediately boosted my confidence. I felt like I could accomplish anything.

Even small treats such as changing your lipstick or experimenting with new cologne can pick up your spirits. I uncovered a new treat for myself that I still enjoy very much, but which does not cost me a lot of money. Every two weeks, I pick up a bouquet of carnations at Walmart. The price is right, and carnations smell lovely. I place them on my desk and they amplify the beauty of my environment. In addition, my pamper priorities are skincare, hair, and pedicure. Once I like a product, I am loyal to that brand, however, I am also open to trying new ones. There are times when I uncover a product that I like even better.

QUESTION 1: Is the idea of pampering yourself something you feel comfortable with, or does it seem like an extravagance you JUST CAN'T AFFORD? Where do you think the belief that you don't deserve or can't afford a personal luxury comes from? How much do you still embrace that belief? What single step can you take today to begin erasing the old tapes that told you that you weren't worthy of pampering and treating yourself well?

QUESTION 2: You deserve to feel good and look great. If you don't feel good and look great – on the inside *and* the outside – it will be apparent in your attitude, and the people you meet will likely reflect that attitude back to you. Write a few affirmations to help you embrace your value so you can start pampering yourself. (Get advice on how to write affirmations here: **the-guided-meditation-site.com/how-to-write-affirmations.html**.)

QUESTION 3: What are some ways you can encourage those around you to embrace the idea of pampering themselves so they can get the same benefits you're receiving from all this self-care?

QUESTION 4: What indulgence would make you happy today?

LIFEHACKS: 40 Tips for Rewriting Your Life

It is all about loving yourself enough to explore some pampering that will leave you feeling special.

TIP #11 – Dance

We know that research supports the benefits of staying active – for both mind and body. Walking daily is great way to get moving and keep your mind active. Yoga, running, hitting the gym, playing tennis or ping pong are even better. Dancing is a fun way to burn calories, too! Have you ever thought of signing up for ballroom dancing? Or, something really fun like belly dancing? If you don't feel like joining a local dance class, then learn at home. You can get great online lessons that will allow you to practice in the comfort of your own home.

QUESTION 1: How often do you get up and just move your body? When the music comes on, are you more likely to tap your foot or hand in rhythm or just listen without moving?

QUESTION 2: If you've ever thought about taking a dance class of any kind and haven't, what's kept you from doing it? Is your reluctance a belief you truly hold, or an excuse because you fear looking foolish? Guess what – pretty much everyone taking a beginner dance class looks foolish. I promise you won't be alone!

QUESTION 3: What kind of dancing might you enjoy? Research a place to take lessons in your area – or look on YouTube. You can find beginner lessons for every form of dance from salsa to hip hop to ballet to ballroom to Irish step – and everything in between.

TIP #12 – Spiritual Renewal

Not every person has a spiritual practice. Many may have grown up in religious households, but have let the traditions of their youth fall away as they grew into adulthood. Spiritual and religious are not the same, either. When I say spiritual, I'm really talking about your personal way of connecting with God, the Universe, a higher consciousness, or simply life itself. We all need a connection and it needs to be renewed and recharged on a regular basis if we want to continue to tap into our own intuition, creativity, and sense of connection to the larger world around us.

Spiritual renewal can come by visiting a church, temple, synagogue, or other place of worship, but it doesn't have to. It can also come through meditation, yoga, dance, music, volunteering, the outdoors, or creative projects. We all need space to refresh and regain our inner connection and focus. Our busy lives can easily disengage our spiritual connection. It is important that we recognize when this happens so that we can get back on track.

QUESTION 1: What, if any, are the spiritual practices from your childhood or young adulthood that you still honor?

QUESTION 2: Do you have a spiritual practice today? If not, what resonates with you as something you can do on a daily, weekly, or monthly basis to reconnect with your higher self?

Reflection, listening to music, spending time outdoors, volunteering, practicing creativity, and appreciating life, make me feel peaceful and complete.

TIP #13 – Create Your Own Zen-like Space or Experience

Seek serenity. Spend time alone in a quiet setting by creating your own Zen-like corner inside or outside your house. Designate this spot as your peaceful space and cherish spending time there. In addition to your Zendo spot in the house, seek ones beyond the house. Spend regular time in a natural setting, admiring your surroundings mindfully. Nature is beautiful, so take time to appreciate it. If you are outside, focus on the designs and colors, studying them with love. Whether it's trees, rocks, animals, or the clouds, give yourself a chance to drink them in. To be in the moment or 'present," you need to be aware of the environment around you. You might visit parks, the zoo, gardens, or even outdoor malls with well-designed landscapes. If you live by the ocean, then you can explore a walk on the beach or sit nearby and listen to the ocean sounds, inhaling the salty air.

I described a trip to one of my personal Zen spots – a Greek monastery spread over acres of lush landscapes, gazebos, and fountains – in my book, **Good Bye Job, Hello Life**: *"I slowly admired the beautifully kept gardens, looking for just the right place to take some photos, pray a little, rest a lot, and just enjoy the stillness. I stopped by each fountain and gazed into the dancing water. Trying to find just the right angle, I took many shots of just the water and then the fountain. Overwhelmed by the beauty, I found it difficult to capture the awe I felt in a photograph. Each sitting area located between palms and trees* *enticed me to spend time there. With a clear mind, I allowed my senses to enjoy nature. Unconcerned about passing time, I let myself enjoy the moment – the peace, the clear blue sky, and the seclusion."*

This passage describes my mindful experience that I captured in photographs. I was fully focusing on the present moment and environment. After this visit, I realized I had identified the best therapy for relaxing and clearing my mind. You, too, should go out and find your bliss. Calmness will help you get in touch with your body and tune into your senses, connecting you to your spirituality. Then, you will be able to hear your inner voice more clearly, focus on something other than your own issues, and ignore your to-do list or feelings of panic. Take a moment and remove yourself from your obstacles and clear your mental trashcan. Daydream. Imagine yourself in your ideal physical setting – a place you could vacation, or even live. If you sit in a Zen place and text, check your emails, or have conversations with another individual, you lose the benefits of experiencing mindfulness.

QUESTION 1: Which corner or room in your home, office, apartment, or yard can you reserve for your Zen space? What has to happen between right now and the minute you can sit in that space to appreciate the quiet and beauty of your surroundings? Clearing clutter? Sweeping? Painting? A new pillow or throw rug? Remember that thrift and resale shops can be a bonanza of wonderful items for your new Zen space – it doesn't have to cost a fortune!

QUESTION 2: How will you make regular time to spend in your new Zen space? Do you have to write it on your calendar or put a reminder on your phone? Maybe you can just go there after breakfast or dinner? Will you be sharing the space with another member of your family – or is this going to be your private space?

QUESTION 3: Get online and do some research – where are the spots in your community you might visit on a regular basis to find some peace, calm, and inspiration. Choose one and mark a date within the next four weeks on your calendar when you will visit.

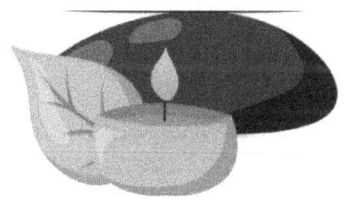

LIFEHACKS: 40 Tips for Rewriting Your Life

Nature is beautiful, so take time to appreciate it.

TIP #14 – Music Therapy

In my book, **Good Bye Job, Hello Life**, I wrote: "*I purchased all kinds of relaxing music. The instrumentals helped me the most, especially slow and peaceful sounds. ... My musical healing process extended to purchasing CDs with actual meditation exercises and positive affirmations. ... I had read somewhere that music can block distractions, boost concentration, and improve moods. I really believe this is true. Whether opera, baroque, classical or various international music, each inspired my creativity. I love many sounds and selecting one depends on what my purpose is at the time.*"

You may already know what kind of music inspires you. If you don't, take the time to discover what works best for you. ITunes is one of the greatest resources – you can purchase music from all over the world. Explore different types of music – there are so many incredible sounds from other cultures that may prove to be your best inspiration. If you ever visit Phoenix, Arizona, be sure to check out the Musical Instrument Museum (MIM). Nationally renowned, this museum displays more than 6,500 various instruments and showcases sounds from around the world. Wearing wireless headphones, you can indulge in many of the global tunes. It's truly an incredible experience. (http://mim.org)

If you are looking for meditation CDs, this website has a large selection: **soundstrue.com.**

QUESTION 1: What are your musical experiences? Did you grow up in a musical family? Was music always on in the background? Or, were you taught that music was a distraction, rather than a necessity in life?

QUESTION 2: What kinds of music do you enjoy? What kinds of music do you avoid at all costs? Why do you like the music you like? Why don't you like the music you find distasteful?

QUESTION 3: How willing are you to go outside your comfort zone to try a new type of music? Would you hear a new band on a friend's recommendation? What might you be missing by limiting yourself to the same old tunes you've known and loved for years? What if your greatest inspiration was just one song away – if only you'd given it a chance?

***Taking time out is a particularly good idea
if you find yourself feeling confused and depressed.***

PART III: Re-Channeling of Energies

This segment is about exploring your authentic self, gaining new perspectives and expanding your experiences.

Re-channeling your energies helps you adjust your attitude and focus on the **new** you and your new goal. Also, it is a great way to uncover your passions, your talents, and perhaps even a new focus you would like to develop in your life. Be open to all opportunities, follow your intuition, and you will find a way to unlock your potential.

Be persistent to unlock your potential...

TIP #15 – Get to Know the Real You

If you're like most people, chances are you've been busy with life and haven't focused a lot of attention on yourself. When we get overly occupied with family, work, and social obligations, we place our needs last. In order to enable yourself to move closer to the next exciting chapter in your life, make self-awareness a priority. Analyze your deepest thoughts.

Start by bringing yourself to a calm, positive state of being. Then research your buried wishes, passions, and desires. Is your life where you want it to be? Do you have an issue you need to resolve or a relationship you need to repair – or release? Do you want to change your career? Or do you want to pursue a passion you've kept hidden since childhood? What do you *really* want to do with your life? **Paying attention to yourself and listening to your inner voice takes some practice.**

QUESTION 1: Write the heading "Who Am I?" on a piece of paper and brainstorm everything you recognize about yourself. Do this in a quiet setting with no distractions. Be still and listen to your authentic thinking. What is your core value?

QUESTION 2: Make a list of all of your talents, characteristics, skills, and unique traits and be proud of all that you are. Include your skills that your teachers, bosses or other people recognized as your strengths.

QUESTION 3: Make a list of skills you would like to improve. What actions can you take to work on enhancing those skills? Classes, Workshops, Volunteering are some ideas.

QUESTION 4: Are there any habits you would like to break? Habits may be hard to break, but it is possible to do it. Look up improvement suggestions online and track your progress.

QUESTION 5: What is your personal branding? What is your uniqueness?

QUESTION 6: What obstacles prevent you from being truly happy?

QUESTION 7: How important is identifying and chasing your dream to you?

QUESTION 8: How can you unleash your ambition and explore all parts of yourself?

QUESTION 9: Study your list. Do you recognize something about yourself you forgot or never paid attention to? Do you have a hidden, untapped talent? What is the first thing on the list you'd like to nurture? What will be the first step you take toward pursuing this new goal?

TIP #16 – Keep a Journal

Keeping a journal is a way to document things you want to remember. Jot down every 'light bulb' thought so that you have it when you are ready to work on it. It's also a great way to get those random thoughts – some of them admittedly negative – out of your head so they no longer occupy your day-to-day life and deter you from pursuing your new life goal.

Your journal can also provide a healing advantage – it's your private place to express your thoughts of anger, fear, or happiness. Looking at a favorite photo when you feel stressed out really helps. Use favorite images, songs, foods, or places in nature to inspire your journaling and your life.

Journaling doesn't have to take a long time – and it can be quite cathartic. You can do it longhand in a book (highly recommended), on your laptop, or even in a notes section on your phone. Getting the thoughts down is the most important aspect of journaling, to be sure, but think about it as a place to unleash your creativity. Use your journal as a scrapbook for your favorite places, quotes, and inspirations. Document your vision and goals.

QUESTION 1: Have you ever kept a journal or diary? How long has it been since you've written on a regular basis?

QUESTION 2: What has held you back from keeping a journal? How can you incorporate it into your daily life?

QUESTION 3: Journals come in all shapes, sizes and colors. Find one that invites you to write into it. Next, try to find a regular time to write in your journal – and, if possible, a dedicated journaling place. Making this a part of your daily routine will give you something to look forward to and create a record of how far you've come on your journey of self-discovery.

Don't be afraid of change. Instead of fighting it, use the energy to adapt to it.

TIP #17 – Travel or Act as a Tourist in Your City

Getting away is a great way to channel your energy. Changing your perspective helps your rejuvenation process. If you can't afford a trip to Paris, consider taking a local daytrip. There might be an interesting place to visit just an hour or two away from your home. A change in setting or a new adventure can do wonders for your attitude. The goal is to take your mind off your current challenge. Do something fun and block your thoughts so you aren't focused on your dilemma.

Pretend you are new in your town and go sightseeing in your own city. Have you ever had an out -of-town guest who wanted to see a local tourist attraction you've never visited because you figure you can go anytime? As residents of our communities, we often ignore the attractions in our home towns. This is the perfect time for you to get off the couch and go explore your community! Remember to check out the souvenir or gift shops. Is there a nice mall with an outdoor café where you can sip coffee or tea and people-watch? This activity will take your mind off your dilemma. Having an alfresco lunch is always fun, providing the climate cooperates.

QUESTION 1: What are three local tourist attractions you've never visited or haven't visited in a long time?

QUESTION 2: Choose a date on the calendar within the next four weeks, and write one of the locations you listed in question 1. Visit it on the chosen date.

QUESTION 3: When you visit, view the attraction from the perspective of an out-of-town tourist. What do you notice? What strikes you as funny, different, or noteworthy? Take a notepad or record notes on your phone. They may later inspire you in a surprising way

QUESTION 4: Do you have a bucket list? No? Why not? Perhaps it is time to start one. What are some of the places you would like to see?

QUESTION 5: Did you ever consider visiting a new, beautifully decorated model home just for fun?

Changing your perspective helps your rejuvenation process.

TIP #18 – Find a Hobby

A hobby is anything you do for fun. You don't get paid to do it – you do it because you enjoy it. Maybe you've never had a hobby because you've been too busy climbing the corporate ladder, raising a family, or staying otherwise occupied with the Adult World. Well, now you've got the time, so seize the moment! Figure out what you would enjoy doing and go for it! Is it bowling, tennis, pottery or photography? Get out of your comfort zone; be willing to experiment and explore. Be brave and open minded and choose an activity you've never done. Get in touch with your inner child.

Besides providing an entertaining opportunity to explore and have fun, hobbies will put you in touch with others who may share your vision and passion.

Start by allotting a half-hour every day or every other day to investigate and explore your new interest. Will you have to invest in any supplies to get started? Try a thrift store or eBay before spending money on brand new equipment. Once you know you're going to stick with your newfound interest, you can always upgrade.

QUESTION 1: What were your hobbies as a child and younger adult?

QUESTION 2: If you've left past hobbies by the wayside, would you like to resume one of those, or seek out a brand new interest?

QUESTION 3: What are activities do you enjoy doing, but never pursued because you didn't have time, it wasn't realistic, grownups don't DO that sort of thing, or you couldn't afford it? Choose one, and then research it at the library or on the internet. Join a Meetup group focused on your hobby.

Get out of your comfort zone; be willing to experiment and explore.

TIP #19 – Expand Your World – Keep on Learning

When was the last time you bothered to learn something for the sheer joy of it? Now is the time to discover this joy. Learning something new will make you feel better about yourself. Have you considered learning a new language, checking out an art class, or attending a cooking class or computer class? Whatever you want to learn, there's probably someone teaching it someplace near you or online. There are many short-term classes available at community colleges, art schools, libraries, community centers, and senior centers. Check Facebook, Craigslist, or Meetup. People post event listings for all kinds of classes on these sites. Khan Academy (khanacademy.org) provides world-class education for anyone, anywhere.

Whatever you do, **NEVER STOP LEARNING**! If you stop stretching your mind, it will literally begin to shrink. Challenge yourself to pursue continuous growth and mind expansion. Not only is this important for self-renewal, but it will enhance your self-esteem, your self-confidence, and your personal innovation efforts. It will also keep you fluent in the latest practices and technology. You need to remain updated on information and the world around. Don't find yourself left behind. Whether you are an entrepreneur or work for corporate America, it is imperative to upgrade your skills continuously.

Over the years, I have made it a practice to attend classes, seminars, and workshops. Whether they are work or hobby-related, they provide inspiration, motivation, new ideas and new skills.

QUESTION 1: What have you always wanted to learn more about?

QUESTION 2: Where might you find a class on this subject in your community? If there's a fee for the class, what can you do to earn a little extra cash to help you pay for the class?

QUESTION 3: If there absolutely isn't a class available close to you, try YouTube. Better yet, get a group of friends together and make your own class based on a good YouTube video. Virtually **anything** you want to learn is available online. Just keep looking!

Mira Tasich

Whatever you do, **_NEVER STOP LEARNING_**!

TIP #20 – Get Your Creativity Flowing

To jumpstart your imagination, take on a creative project – even if you are a little reluctant. Organize those family photos sitting in boxes. Visit a scrapbook store where you can find all kinds of cute enhancements to add to your album. Get out and take some photos, and then frame and display them. Create something! Can you sew, crochet or knit? Visit a thrift store to look for some yarn or fabric. Have fun with watercolors. Try oil painting, too. Make some greeting cards. Use recycled items from around your house – wrapping paper, the Sunday funnies, photos and words from magazines to create a montage. Pick up a coloring book. Try wood carving.

Regardless of what the task is, take some time to explore your creative side. Everyone has some creativity even if it seems hidden. You just need to try different things until you tap into something that resonates with you. And you never know when a creative pursuit will awaken your inspirations or imagination. Visiting an art show, a gift shop, or a museum can be all the impetus you need to trigger an idea for an exciting project. Remember, be open minded. Gazing in the sky or getting out into nature feels great, but practicing creativity evokes healing powers as well as new ideas. Perhaps you can find a way to combine both. Just keep experimenting until you find out what works for you. If you run out of options, a visit to a creative place like Hobby Lobby, Michael's, or Barnes & Noble might spark an inspiration.

The therapeutic effect of a creative project is often overlooked. Creativity drove my skill expansion, led me to uncovering my true passions, and helped me alleviate my daily stresses. In addition, I used my creativity to solve problems I have faced over the years.

QUESTION 1:   What have you always wanted to create?

QUESTION 2:   Do not stop at one. Select several creative projects. Taking local community classes is a great way to explore many options. Are you ready to experiment?

QUESTION 3:   Are you open to exploring all of your ideas without letting your inner voice discourage you?

QUESTION 4: Visit a gift shop, a book store or a library. Can you pick up a magazine or a book that you normally do not read? Stretch your imagination. You might come up with an innovative idea.

QUESTION 5: Did you ever consider taking a cooking class?

Color the picture as you wish.....

TIP #21 – Volunteer

Americans get involved in volunteering activities primarily through school or church projects. But this is the perfect time for you to look for a cause that matters to you and find a way to help out – to give back. As of 2014, the value of one volunteer hour to an organization was, on average, $23.07. Understandably, many, many organizations are looking for volunteers. Besides helping make a difference, volunteering can give you the chance to get out of the house, uncover a previously undiscovered career interest, boost your personal sense of worthiness, or find inspiration by exploring new people and environments. The fact is that giving feels GOOD.

Take a look online for ideas about where and how to volunteer in your community. **VolunteerMatch.com** is a great site that can help pair people who want to help with agencies, schools, and organizations.

In my book, **Good Bye Job, Hello Life**, Chapter 26 titled,

"Rewriting My Life Story", under the Birth of a New Hobby paragraph, I write: *"After a little over a month volunteering in the beautiful gift shop at the hospital and admiring all the knickknacks, including jewelry, that they were selling, I started thinking about creating an inspirational bracelet."* This thought was the beginning of something I never imagined I could do: jewelry design. By admiring a collection of their displayed jewelry, I got the urge to create something on my own. Not only did I uncover a talent, but shortly after I also found a paying position for my dream company. At first I was just happy to contribute to humanity, network, meet new people, and start building my confidence back, but volunteering gave me so much more. I uncovered one of my passions, sealed my interest in helping people, and turned my life around. The gift shop inspired me because it was a showcase of creativity items, but also it was fun interacting with people.

QUESTION 1: What, outside of your immediate friends and family, is important to you? Does a cause, an interest, an artistic pursuit mean a lot to you? Do you have a friend or family member suffering from a particular illness or condition? Have you always loved the theatre or the ballet? Would you enjoy working with your dog to help a veteran or an abused child?

QUESTION 2: If the idea of volunteering is new to you – or you haven't done it in a l-o-n-g time, how do you think giving back of your time and talent could make a difference for those you helped? More importantly, how do you think giving back could make a difference in YOUR life?

QUESTION 3: Go to **VolunteerMatch.com** or a similar site and find a place that does work that matters to you and can use your help. Call them up and offer your services. If you're timid, invite a friend to join you.

QUESTION 4: Did you ever consider volunteering for the company where you want to work?

QUESTION 5: Be sure to write about your volunteer experiences in your journal. You may be amazed at how your perspective changes over time.

LIFEHACKS: 40 Tips for Rewriting Your Life

Besides helping make a difference, volunteering can give you the chance to get out of the house, uncover a previously undiscovered career interest, boost your personal sense of worthiness, or find inspiration by exploring new people and environments.

TIP #22 – Spread Kindness

In 2002, Jeannette and Dean Maré lost their youngest son to a freak illness. As you might expect, their pain was unimaginable and they didn't know how they'd live through it. Slowly, they began incorporating coping strategies into their lives. Part of coping included art therapy – making ceramic bells, which they crafted in a backyard studio with friends. The therapeutic effect of working with clay was amazing as was the power of being surrounded by people talking and working toward a common goal. The Marés decided to make hundreds of the bells and distribute them randomly throughout their community to encourage the kindness that they had come to depend on to get through each day. On the first anniversary of their son's passing, hundreds of Ben's Bells were distributed throughout Tucson, Arizona, hung randomly in trees, on bike paths, and in parks with a written message asking people to take one home and pass on the kindness.

The ripple effect that followed was wonderful and startling. Now, people around Tucson, the state of Arizona, the U.S., and across the globe are painting Ben's Bells to help spread a singular message: Be Kind. Learn more about this amazing project here: **bensbells.org**.

A kind act, no matter how big or small, is a wonderful thing. When kindness is passed on, it benefits both you and the recipient. Giving a compliment, saying hello, and smiling are small acts of kindness that can refresh your day and make someone else's. And, the best part is that they are free! Making a small donation, giving an item you no longer need or use, or hand-crafting a gift for another person are all great ways to make a big difference with minimal effort.

Empathy and kindness have been a part of me as long as I can remember. Growing up in Eastern Europe, I was taught by my grandmother to smile and say hello to everyone. I apply my gestures of kindness in my daily personal and business lives, and they come from my heart without any expectations of being repaid. However, in most cases there is always some type of a reward or gratification. I can recall one of my recent karmic gratifications.

As I chatted with one of my friends who was unemployed at the time, I learned that she was on the way to a different city for a job interview and had no cash. I looked at my wallet, found $40, and gave it to her. Few days later, I was on my way to Portland, Oregon, to do a TV interview. Since it was important to have nicely styled hair, I stopped by the home of a friend who had volunteered to do my hair. It happened to be Valentine's Day, and after styling my hair, she offered me a gift bag. Rushing to get to my flight, I did not even open it until I was waiting to board the flight at the gate. I looked into the bag and found a small box and a card. Both left me breathless. My friend had made me earrings in my favorite color, the color I had chosen to wear on my interview. Once I opened the card, I found $40 in it, with a note: "Have a nice lunch on me." I was amazed. A few days later, I happened to notice a new scratch ticket at Wal-Mart and decided to try my luck for fun. I won $40.

QUESTION 1: When was the last time someone did you an unexpected kindness? How did their action make you feel?

QUESTION 2: Is your natural tendency to do small kindnesses for others, or does the idea of these kinds of gestures feel foreign to you? There's no right or wrong answer – it just helps to understand if this is a more native behavior, or something you will have to work to cultivate?

QUESTION 3: If small kindness gestures feel a bit awkward or forced, you will need to practice before they become second nature. Start small. Try smiling at the people you encounter in your daily life – the grocery store, post office, gas station attendant, coworkers, family members. Will it feel weird at first? Yep. Do it anyway. Then add a hello, perhaps a wave. People may wonder what's gotten into you. Let them wonder. Just keep spreading kindness. Before you know it, you will notice strangers making the same kinds of gestures to you. Your life will be richer for it.

QUESTION 4: When was the last time you listened to someone's story with empathy?

TIP #23 – Expand Your Vision

Do you want a change, but still have no idea where to begin? Volunteering did not open any new horizons or provide innovative inspirations for you. Give it some time. Could that new hobby be turned into a profitable venture? Perhaps one of your passions could grow into a career or develop into your own business. For the time being, however, finances deter that possibility. Be patient. Make a plan, and take consistent action – regardless of how big or small – toward bringing your desired outcome to reality. If you remain unsure about what you would like to do, think back to your childhood. Don't give up trying to expand your vision and imagination.

Perhaps an aptitude test would help give you a better idea of what you are most suited for. The question these tests ask is: **What would you love to do if you did not have to work for**

a living? If you are not working at the moment, you may need to find an interim job to pay the bills. That's fine – but don't let it deter you. Do your temporary job with as much passion as you can muster, and that positive attitude will roll over as you continue to focus on landing the dream job you really want.

If you work for a good company, but are getting stale in your current assignment, think about ways you can enhance your position. Be in charge of your own development. Seek additional tasks that will increase your skills, volunteer for various internal groups to expand your network, and take advantage of any development programs that might be available.

Many Meet up groups cater to events for singles to help them meet someone 'special.' In addition, museums and clubs often plan activities geared for networking with other singles such as cocktail parties, hikes, book reviews, lectures or movies. Finding a partner with a shared interest is the first step to a solid relationship.

QUESTION 1: What led you to seek the job you now have – or were recently separated from?

QUESTION 2: What is your favorite thing about that job? What is your least favorite thing about it?

QUESTION 3: Write a description of your job – focusing on the things you love about it.

QUESTION 4: If you don't love your job, why are you worrying about the thought of losing it? Isn't this the opportunity of a lifetime to make a course correction to pursue a job you truly want, one that taps into all of your skills and challenges you to grow both personally and professionally?

QUESTION 5: If you didn't have to worry about getting paid for your work, what would you spend more/all of your time doing?

QUESTION 6: For people desiring to meet that special someone: Write a detailed description of what that person would look like.

LIFEHACKS: 40 Tips for Rewriting Your Life

TIP # 24 – Passion Meets You...

...if you let it. And when you are in the right frame of mind and open to new experiences, chances are greater that you will uncover your passion. Your mental attitude will help you succeed at finding your passion, but it applies to *everything* you do. Your attitude is one of the critical keys to success in seeing any project through.

Finding your passion can be a long, difficult journey filled with detours and potholes. Sometimes career and other obligations may have steered you astray so the pathway to acting upon your passion - not just thinking about it - can be difficult and stressful.

When I was in sixth grade, I loved to write and was interested in learning about photography. I signed up for after school programs focused on these interests. However my move to U.S. and learning a new culture and language impelled me to find a well paying job and ignore my passions. After I was laid off, I realized writing was an important outlet for me so I patiently followed my intuition.

QUESTION 1: Do you have an attitude of "I want to do that!" or "I want to try that!" or would you rather pull the covers back over your head and stay in bed all day?

QUESTION 2: Perhaps you have been doing the wrong things for far too long. Little or big, what would excite you to jump out of bed and greet the day with a smile? Don't let others' opinions or a low salary deter you. If you could do ANYTHING tomorrow, what would you most like to do with your day?

QUESTION 3: Are you afraid to pursue the unknown? Perhaps you dismiss your talents before they have a chance to reach the external world. Write a story of your life living your passions. Imagine how it would be if you were to use the talent you were born with but have not had a chance to pursue.

Mira Tasich

Part IV: Life & Career Rejuvenation

It's time to take a look at your current life and career and – hopefully – incorporate your (newly discovered) passion into it. Were you able to get any hints from the prior steps? Perhaps you need assistance in making your evaluation. What do leaders do when they need help? They delegate! I located this site couple of years ago and I was really impressed. A credentialed coach and career development expert, Deborah Brown-Volkman offers many resources on her website. In addition to her results-oriented Career Coaching programs for those who want a new job, new career, or a new way to flourish in today's hectic workplace, as well as, wellness programs, she offers a free 30 minute phone session. Meet Deborah Brown-Volkman, President, Surpass Your Dreams, Inc. Top International Coach Federation (ICF) Career Coach, Professional Certified Coach (PCC) & Certified Wellness Coach (CWC) **SurpassYourDreams.com**.

Mira Tasich

Life

**Life is like a canvas...
As you pick the brush
Decide on a color palette,
What technique to use,
Mastery you turn it into...
It's totally up to you.**

TIP #25. Redefine/Reinvent Your Purpose

This is a holistic, three-step process. Be sure to engage in all the steps. Don't skip any of them because they're hard. Making a change is difficult – but you're committed, aren't you? You probably wouldn't still be reading this book if you weren't. Making this change – or confirming that the path you're on is the right one – will lead you to greater fulfillment in the next phase of your life. Take as long as you need to figure things out.

1. Determine what your passion is (see tip #24). Be open minded and allow yourself to explore all possibilities. Is it the career have now, or do you want a change? Is your passion entirely outside of work – a hobby, perhaps? Is it something you still have yet to uncover? Be as resourceful as you can and need to be. Do not stop trying – be persistent.

2. Think about how you would like to impact the world. Self

awareness is very important. What are your skills? What do you enjoy doing? What are you good at? If you need to gain new skills, you can make a plan to do so later on. Be flexible so that you can look at your problem, challenge, or issue with new eyes. How would a person from another country – or an alien from another planet – view your situation? What would **you** do if you already knew the answer to your dilemma? Go everywhere to research ideas, get a fresh perspective, and think differently about the situation.

3. Align your vision, passion and purpose and develop your strategy depending on your personal career choice and financial needs. Expand your vision and strategy continuously (to start, see Tip #23). As you commence rewriting your own story, depending on whether you are looking for a temporary job, career, or hobby, do not stop exploring various aspects of creativity. Whether your interest might be hidden in artistic pursuits or not, creativity promotes a great state of mind and perspective that enables you to come up with different solutions needed in other areas of your life.

QUESTION 1: On a scale of 1 to 10 (1 being the lowest and 10 being the highest), how fulfilled are you doing the work you've been doing? How fulfilled are you in the relationship undergoing upheaval? How fulfilled have you been with life in general?

QUESTION 2: Looking back at your journal entries and thinking back to the prior tips and your experiences with them, what new interests and passions have you discovered that you may never have realized you had before? How strong are those passions? Which one could be THE thing you want to focus on, going forward?

QUESTION 3: What steps could you take today to begin moving in a direction of focusing on your new passion? Costs aside, education aside, appropriateness aside – how ready are you to take that first step? What's holding you back?

QUESTION 4: Are there any skills you need to learn before you can plan out your new purpose or chase your dreams?

QUESTION 5: Write some affirmations to help you move past the blocks and take that first step. Seek help if you need it.

TIP #26 – Develop Your Plan of Action

Are you finally ready to turn a new page? Have you explored all of your options and opportunities? If your plan is to get a new job, do you know what type of job you want? Do you want to be an entrepreneur? If you're thinking about starting your own business, be sure to do your research first. Many cities have local organizations staffed by retired executives who provide free guidance and hold classes for people who want to start their own businesses.

Is the new position you're seeking similar to something you've done in the past, or are you thinking about moving into a new profession entirely? Have you found a passion that you want to turn into a career? Will you require additional education? How much time, realistically, will you need before you can pursue the opportunity you really want? Do you have to move out of state?

When the automotive industry went through job cuts and challenges in 2006, I decided to seek employment in Phoenix, Arizona. Once I landed a position in the aerospace industry, my husband and I had less than two weeks to make this huge move. He was able to obtain a company transfer for his position and that made things a little easier; however, leaving family and friends was not easy. Flexibility and overcoming fear of the unknown paid off. This move ended up being my life defining moment. Not only that I ended up working for a company I loved, but also, I uncovered my passion that initiated an exciting transformation. It all started with an 8-month long contract position that many people would not even consider as a reason to move out of state. At times taking a risk pays off. My husband did have a full-time position – having that income helped me make my decision to take a risky position.

QUESTION 1: First, you need to decide if you will pursue work in your current industry or make a radical change to something brand new.

QUESTION 2: Once you know the career you have chosen, you need to put your plan on paper. What are the 10 most important steps you need to take to land that job or start a business?

QUESTION 3: What is a realistic timeline for starting a new job, opening a business, or turning a passion into a career? Build in some padding for unexpected life occurrences, but give yourself a realistic deadline. Goals without timelines are merely wishes.

QUESTION 4: Put your actions steps on your calendar and then honor those dates with yourself as intently as you would an obligation to a client or your boss.

QUESTION 5: Write down some specific goals, both short-term and long-term.

You may have all the tools and lessons, but you are the only one who can re-write your story!

Are you finally ready to turn a new page?

Mira Tasich

Your attitude is one of the critical keys to success in seeing any project through.

TIP #27 – Go into Action

Assuming you have to work and need to get a job, when was the last time you updated your résumé? If it's been more than a year and you have changed jobs or received a promotion since the last version, it's time to revise it. Once it's done, review it again. If you have the budget, you might consider a hiring a professional résumé writer, like those at Career Pros. They are not only aware of the latest styles and contents employers are seeking in today's résumés, but they will also help you craft a cover letter virtually guaranteed to get you an interview.

Finalize the master copy of your résumé, and modify/personalize it for each position you are applying for. Create your portfolio of recommendations and references. Then take the time to research, research, research. Spend time reviewing which positions are opening and in what industries. Be sure you are able to articulate your transferable skills if you are looking to make a jump from one industry to another. Be certain to update your social media accounts, especially LinkedIn. Stay in touch with your previous coworkers. Submit applications daily. Include cover letters when possible because you can allow your personality to shine through. Don't stop until you get an interview and a job offer.

QUESTION 1: How many opportunities can you research daily? Are you checking companies' career portals, job boards, and social networking sites?

QUESTION 2: Are you identifying job recruiters that could help your search? Are you locating career fairs that you can attend?

QUESTION 3: What are three steps you can take to increase a successful outcome? What can you do to stay on track?

TIP #28 – Socialize/Network/Search for Support

Long-term isolation is probably not a good idea when you are trying to make a change. Now is a good time to get connected. Get in touch with or visit family and friends. But be careful. Stay away from people who mean well but cannot empathize. Avoid spending time with folks who emphasize your current obstacles or help you remain stuck in a negative thought pattern. If they ask you what your plans are or how you are going to survive, tell them you're taking some time to figure it out. If they're positive, they will encourage you and champion whatever new path you decide to pursue. If change is scary for them, the new you may not meet their expectations and you will likely hear words of discouragement. Say a hasty goodbye to these people.

As you uncover your new profession or hobby, seek out like-minded people who encourage these activities. If you cannot get this kind of support from family and friends, don't expect it from them. Instead, join local organizations, Meetups, or associations will help you experience the encouragement of being among people with common interests and goals. Connect with people in the area of your interest to learn about any potential opportunities.

QUESTION 1: Who is your Number 1 fan, the person who will cheer you on no matter what the circumstance? He or she should be the first one you turn to for encouragement.

QUESTION 2: If you don't have a Number 1 fan, who are the people in your life who generally encourage you? They could be family, neighbors, friends, friend of friends, your spiritual community, a social group, or mentor. Spend time with them and soak up the good vibrations they emit as you communicate your new plans and goals.

QUESTION 3: If you lack a supportive community, it's time to get one! Where might like-minded people meet on a regular basis? Look for Meetups, spiritual communities, volunteer organizations, civic groups, or cultural activities. If you're feeling a bit alone in the world, someone else is, too – find them so you can support each other!

LIFEHACKS: 40 Tips for Rewriting Your Life

Escaping your comfort zone may pave your way to bigger and better things.

TIP #29 – Look the Part

It is great to be ourselves. However, when it comes to getting ahead in your career, it pays to be aware of your image and the impression you make when people see you especially if you are in a professional role or trying to obtain one. You need to make sure you look polished and confident. If you showed up in your sweats, ripped jeans, or something resembling pajamas, what kind of message would you portray to your co-workers? You may love your look, but be honest and place yourself in the other person's shoes. Does it really support the message you are trying to convey? In today's competitive world, you want to increase your advantage, not reduce it. Find a look that reflects comfort and style according to the situation. For people on a budget, there are many resale shops that make great clothes affordable.

If you are in a professional field, it also pays to work on your communication skills. Make sure you speak thoughtfully, enunciate, use proper grammar, and maintain eye contact. Regardless of your profession, it is always a good thing to examine how you act and appear to the rest of the world. **You** may be overly loud and unwittingly annoy others. **You** may listen a bit carelessly, interrupting without letting others finish their thoughts. We may assume everyone wants to know more about us than we should probably share – especially on a first meeting. A little self-awareness about how we look and act is healthy so that we can work on improving ourselves to make the best impression.

QUESTION 1:   What impression would you like to make on a new acquaintance? When you step back to review your appearance and mannerisms as objectively as you can, how well do you think you convey that impression?

QUESTION 2: Ask someone – or several people – you trust for honest feedback on how you come across. Ask people you know to be honest, but kind. Do their answers surprise you? Have they given you good information that triggers ideas about ways to improve your appearance or mannerisms?

QUESTION 3:   If you're not sure where to start, head to your local library or check out YouTube. Makeover experts abound in all areas from confidence to interviewing skills to speaking skills to style and dress.

A little self-awareness about how we look and act is healthy.

V. Stay in the CEO Lane of Your Life

Whether you are re-writing your story or just rejuvenating your current life, these tools and tips will guide you and help you be successful in many areas of your life.

As noted in the introduction, you hold the answers to reconciling your dilemma. No one else does. You are responsible for your thoughts and actions. You have the POWER to create a happy life. You may seek help and support, obtain ideas, learn new approaches, but ultimately, you are the CEO in charge of pulling it all together and making it work. And, only you can uncover your passions, potential, and possibilities.

Once you find the best tips for you, the key is to stay on track. Do not let anything detour your journey to controlling your life. Setbacks occur, but stay in the CEO lane of your life.

Mira Tasich

You are responsible for your thoughts and actions.

Summarize your favorite affirmations

Mira Tasich

Color by numbers

TIP #30 – Living with the "New Normal"

We need to accept change in our life. Whether the shift is from employed to unemployed, employee to entrepreneur, or married to divorced, single to married, change is difficult. We must constantly work to find our own way and adjust our attitudes. If you change your career and find yourself uncomfortable in your new role, join industry associations or civic organizations to give you the opportunity to network with other professionals in your field. If you've recently rejoined the "singles" realm, look for a supportive Meetup or perhaps a similar group within your spiritual community. It is always uplifting to be among people who share a common interest.

We share more with others than we think we do. Finding

others to connect to is fairly easy nowadays with social media. Facebook has plenty of groups to suit every taste and desire; LinkedIn has a multitude of professional and industry-specific groups; and Craigslist can also help you meet people with similar interests in your area. Use caution about sharing too much online.

When I first became a published author, the new title made me uncomfortable. It was easier for me to write a book than it was thinking of my "new normal" as an author. Immediately, I joined a local association of authors and at the first meeting I met approximately 30 individuals I liked and could share thoughts with. They were at different experience levels, but I walked away with additional knowledge, inspiration and confidence.

QUESTION 1: How are you viewing your new role in life – whether it's temporary or likely longer-lasting? Are you embracing it, or finding yourself continually wishing things were "the way they used to be?"

QUESTION 2: It can definitely be challenging to find yourself suddenly thrust into a "new normal" – particularly when your old normal was so comfortable. Meeting people in similar circumstances might help you adjust to your new role, position, or location. Where are the best places to meet those people?

QUESTION 3: If meeting new people is particularly challenging for you, what affirmation can you write to help you get past the fear? A quick search on YouTube for "fear of meeting new people" returned 7.2 million results! Make some time today to watch just one video that resonates with you and spend the rest of the week applying what you learn. Journal about your experience.

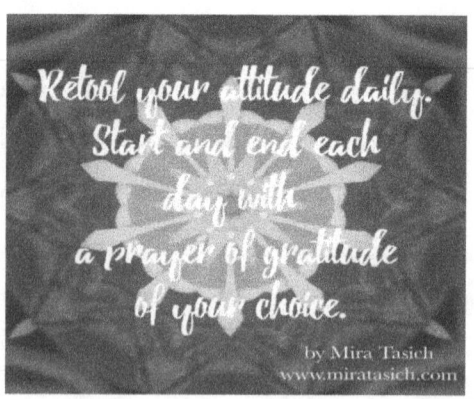

Take a coloring break........

TIP #31 – Stay Positive

An unfortunate number of people like to think of themselves as victims and spend their valuable energy dwelling on negativity again and again and again. Rather than joy, pessimism, sadness, or helplessness are their default emotions.

Stop! Stop! Stop!

First – negative thinking can make you physically ill. You might be surprised to learn how many chronic illnesses (including cancer) are related to our own thoughts – things we, alone, control. Second, stop blaming other people for the position you are in. Take responsibility for your own destiny. You cannot wait for someone to come to your doorstep to rescue you. You've got to roll up your sleeves and create your own personal rescue plan.

Your perspective is important. If you are not a positive person, challenge yourself to become one. Go back to your affirmations as many times as you need to. Find a hypnosis program to help you change your thinking. Watch comedies and positive videos instead of spending hours on Facebook envying the lives of others. Work on looking at the world in a more positive manner. Spend **your** energy creating the life **you** want and deserve.

And if something knocks you down, get up, rejuvenate, and keep moving. Be open to seizing opportunities that come your way – you may find your journey leading you to places you never envisioned at the start. Eliminate negative character traits like jealousy and envy. We should all eliminate these from our lives because all they do is breed self-doubt, insecurity, and lack of self-worth. They create hurt and division and drive people away from us. Identify these feelings in your life and work on eliminating them, especially if they are causing friction with your partner.

QUESTION 1: On a scale of 1 to 10 (1 being the extremely negative and 10 being the extremely positive), how positive or negative are you most of the time? Is your default to see the glass as half-full or half-empty?

QUESTION 2: Maybe you don't even notice how often you complain – *start paying attention!* If you tend to want to shame, blame, or complain instead of taking responsibility for what's going on in your own life, when did that pattern start? Answering honestly will lead you to a happier, more fulfilled life.

QUESTION 3: When you catch yourself feeling sorry for yourself, blaming others for your problems, or feeling like the whole world is out to get you, stop. Breathe. Take a moment to ask yourself what small thing you can do to reframe that perception and see it from a more neutral perspective. Not a positive one – just a neutral one...

QUESTION 4: What steps can you take today to stop being a victim, a whiner, or a complainer? What actions can you take to empower yourself and take responsibility for having a good day?

**Your perspective is important. If you are not a positive person,
challenge yourself to become one.**

TIP #32 – Be Flexible

Today, the ability to remain flexible is one of the most important qualities. Change is the only constant, so we must know – or learn – how to adapt to it. Remaining focused on the past or protecting your comfort zone only adds to your frustration, ultimately increasing your problems. You've probably heard it already – work on being "agile." If there is a new opportunity, go for it! If you have a chance to work in a different city, why not move? Experiencing a new environment might be the perfect thing for you right now.

Feeling slightly uncomfortable forces you to grow professionally and personally. The challenges and failures actually teach you more than a routine, comfortable existence will because they demand new knowledge and create new experiences. If we hang on to our comfort level, we can expect to stay in place and even fall behind. Agility and flexibility are skills that allow you to embrace new situations and discover the best way to deal with them.

If change is something you fear, you may need to build your flexibility muscles slowly. Begin by taking a new path home from work. Order something different from the menu at your favorite restaurant. Write something with your non-dominant hand. Reverse your morning ritual, starting with the last thing you normally do before you leave the house and ending with the first thing you usually do. Build from there.

QUESTION 1: On a scale of 1 to 10 (1 being unbendable and 10 being as flexible as a Chinese gymnast), how flexible are you? Are there certain areas of life where you're more prone to bending, or do you like things the way they are across the board?

QUESTION 2: What is your typical response when a change occurs that is beyond your control? Does it depend on the type or severity of the situation?

QUESTION 3: What are three steps you can take to increase your adaptability and to anticipate change eagerly?

QUESTION 4: If you learn about an opportunity to meet someone new or work on a new task, what is you criteria to even consider this change? What are the steps you can take to welcome experimenting with unknown prospects?

Feeling slightly uncomfortable forces you to grow professionally and personally. The challenges and failures actually teach you more than a routine, comfortable existence will because they demand new knowledge and create new experiences.

TIP #33 – Create Your Own Uplifting Drill

To Overcome Doubt & Improve Your Self-Esteem & Confidence

Expect doubt to show up. Overcoming doubt is very difficult, especially if you are in a new role or environment. We are often our own worst enemies, quickly chastising ourselves when things don't go our way or something challenging happens to our livelihood. This ego-driven response tears down our self-esteem and helps keep us stuck. Make every effort to avoid this habit. Create a list of all of your accomplishments and skills – and take a look at the list daily. Journals are great for this type of effort. In moments when your internal "negative" little voice speaks to you, don't let it win. Pull out your journal. Remind yourself of your skills and don't ignore your past successes. Keep your goals in front of you (both short and long term) so you can remain passionate about completing them.

My journey to a new location - Arizona, to a new career and to a new avocation born out of passion has compelled me to live more fully and more aware. Blending my two careers with my personal life is challenging. It requires persistence and personal sacrifice. In moments of doubt, I pull out my list of accomplishments and goals. I have learned to change my internal voice to say, "I can do this" instead of "No, this will never work."

QUESTION 1: You've likely heard that the first step toward correcting a problem is realizing that you have a problem. Pay attention to how often you use negative self-talk to berate yourself for causing the situation you find yourself in now.

QUESTION 2: Now that you've started noticing your negative self-talk, what can you do to change it to positive, reinforcing inner commentary? Some people place a rubber band on their wrists and snap it every time they find themselves thinking a negative thought. Others create an affirmation they use to replace the negative comment.

QUESTION 3: Pay attention to the number of times you say positive things to yourself. As the number of negatives comes down, the number of positives should increase!

QUESTION 4: What are some fun items that you can keep in your area that would inspire your creativity and mood?

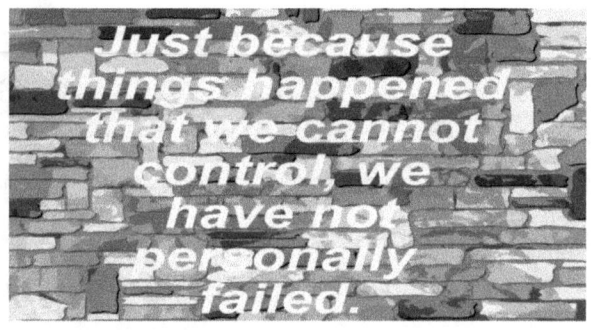

Remind yourself of your skills and don't ignore your past successes.

TIP #34 – Build Your Inspirational Boost File

Think about people who inspire you. What have they done to earn your respect? Why do you feel a connection with them? Is this person someone who achieved a position, title, or accomplishment you would like to earn for yourself? Is it someone whose talent you appreciate? Or, does a particular place inspire you? Is it a dream house that you would perhaps like to own someday? Maybe it's a piece of music or a painting you've seen in a museum. Perhaps it is the sound of children singing and giggling. Everyone is inspired by something different. There is no right or wrong – just work at identifying the people and things that inspire you. **Keep an eye on the end result of what you are trying to achieve.** Create your reminder: it could be a poster board, chalk board, journal reference. Let it be visible to you.

QUESTION 1: Take notes in your journal about the person,

place or thing that inspires you. What qualities do you admire? How does seeing or talking to that person make you feel? What have you learned by reading about them or watching a biopic? What's different for you when you visit an inspirational place or piece of art? How are you connected to the person, place or thing that inspires you?

QUESTION 2: What, specifically, are you inspired to do after basking in the glow or your source of inspiration? Write a chapter in the novel you never knew you wanted to write? Take a class to pursue a career you didn't even know existed? Visit a country on the other side of the world? How can you channel all of that inspiration toward finding – and living – your passion?

QUESTION 3: Whether or not you're keeping a journal, get a cork board and pin photos on it of the person, place, or thing that most inspires you. Keep your inspiring images easily visible. As you look at them daily, put your passionate and creative wishes out into the Universe.

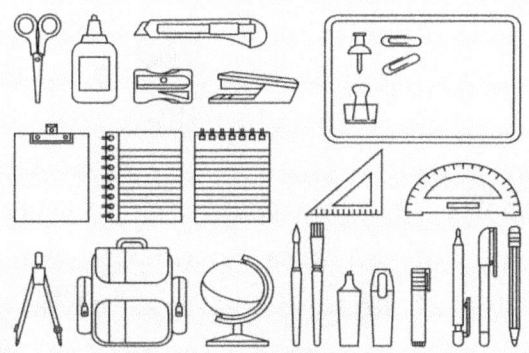

Everyone is inspired by something different. There is no right or wrong – just work at identifying the people and things that inspire you.

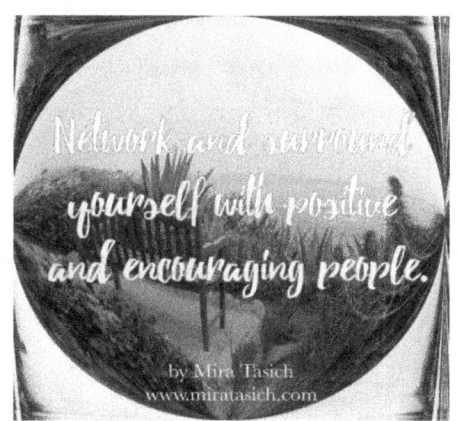

TIP #35 – Embrace Diversity (Yours and Others)

How comfortable are you with who you are? And how comfortable are you with those around you – particularly those who are "different" from you? We all come from various backgrounds, ethnicities, and cultures. At times, these differences are apparent, and perhaps make some of us uncomfortable. But being different is cool. Take time to get to know others. You may discover more similarities than differences.

If you ever feel out of place just remember, it is your thinking, not necessarily that of those around you. Sometimes we commit an unintentional, but embarrassing faux pas. Learn to laugh at yourself and grow from that embarrassing moment. Don't take yourself so seriously, and do not waste time feeling out of place. You might be the one with a unique style; the others are just followers. Get to know the person on the exercise bike next to you who comes from a different background or ethnicity – hear his or her story. It will probably fascinate you!

When I first came to United States I felt out of place. A heavy accent and cultural difference made me aware that I was unique. Those days I viewed my diversity as a weakness and embarrassment. As I made an effort to blend with my new culture, I became a blend of both cultures. Many traditions that did not fit my new lifestyle and goals were discarded - instead I welcomed new ones. I realize now that my multi-cultural facet and experience of working with different ethnicities molded me into a richer person. I recognize the advantage of being diverse and I celebrate it. My divergent ways turned out to be great for creativity, innovation, as well as, rejuvenating my career and life.

QUESTION 1: Is it easy or challenging for you to interact with people different from you? What causes you anxiety? Try to identify what it is. Is it language, culture, race, age, education level, gender, physical ability, sexual preference, religious or political affiliation, or something else? Once you pinpoint the discomfort, find out more about it and see if knowledge helps improve your comfort level.

QUESTION 2: All of us exhibit fear, apprehension, and even prejudice to some degree, regardless of how hard we work to overcome it. What do you think drives an innate fear of the other?

QUESTION 3: What steps can you take to reach out to someone "different" – particularly a person from the group you referred to in your answer to Question 1 – and try to get to know something about them that will give you a sense of common ground, common purpose, and/or common passion?

Regardless of our uniqueness: We are the CEOs, the shareholders, and the employees of our own destinies....

Different

Different, I may be...
And that is fine with me
I am unique, free as a bird to fly
I was brought to this earth for a reason
It took a while, but I finally know why
I live, I love, I feel, I cry...
My struggles reflect good intention,
I dream and create, just trying to survive
Beauty of nature is my passion
Different, I may be, but I am
Just like every person alive.

TIP #36 – Retool Your Attitude Continuously

Attitude retooling is a continuous process, just like learning, especially when you're facing a significant life change. In order to remain open to changing your mindset, thoughts, beliefs, positions – and life, itself, you must expand your knowledge and experiences. You cannot remain set in beliefs influenced by your cultural upbringing, negative experiences, world crises, or your present environment.

If you really believe in what you trying to accomplish, you must be ready to eliminate some negative traits and adopt new ones that will complement your new goal. Learn how to adjust your focus and be willing to learn and adapt continuously.

When I was going through a very difficult time after a lay-off, I adopted a habit that I still practice. I start and end each day by saying my own personal prayer which is a list of the things I am grateful for and a list of items I need help with. Mornings I set the stage to have a positive day and evenings I create a calm state to help me fall asleep quickly. This habit helps me reflect on my day and end it positively so I am ready for tomorrow.

QUESTION 1: How is your present outlook/attitude serving you, in terms of helping you adjust to your new life situation?

QUESTION 2: If you're still tending to lean toward the negative – hating or resisting your new situation, wishing things could just be the way they used to be, or spending lots of time wallowing in sadness, what can you do TODAY to remake your attitude?

QUESTION 3: Think of three people you admire from any time in history. Look up their biographies on Wikipedia or Bio.com. Chances are good that at some point, they suffered an adversity – perhaps a big one. What was it about their outlook or attitude that enabled them to do so? How can you model their perspectives about life to embrace this change and view it as the chance to live your passion?

TIP #37 – Realign Your Actions to Retain Balance

Any new start requires focus and positive energy. Life is full of distractions, so it is easy to get off-track at times. Staying on course takes persistence, which is fueled by having a passion for your goal. Committing to yourself and what you want – going all in – is truly the key. It may be easy enough to decide what you want to do next in life, but staying there can be a challenge. Make sure to find your balance. Find the courage to make decisions to help you live a peaceful life while pursuing your dreams.

No one can afford stress in their daily routine – and now, while you're carving out a new pattern, is the time to create the balance you need to remain calm and focused. Schedule your priorities instead of prioritizing your schedule. Always ensure your personal security – physically, mentally, and spiritually – and make sure your environment supports your personal and professional growth. As much as possible, avoid negative people and negative situations.

I have learned to reduce the time I listen to the news and have stopped watching violent shows. Neither encourages my creativity nor helps me achieve my goals. Continually realigning my actions to encourage both aspects of my life has become my norm. To make the best use of my limited time, many low-ranking chores fall off my to-do list. I remember my grandmother ironing everything and my mother folding her towels a certain way. That type of focus is the last thing on my mind. Who cares how the linens and towels line up in the closet? I am more inspired to create and inspire other people with my creations. Of course doing this plus having a full time job that I love and need to pay the bills keeps me busy.

QUESTION 1: When you think about your past habits and patterns, did you tend to be balanced, geared toward career, or focused on your family's wants and needs? How often did you take time for yourself – to do the things you truly wanted to do?

QUESTION 2: As you make plans for this life change – be it a new job, a new business, a new relationship, or a move to a new place – what steps can you take now to create a balanced life affording you plenty of time to focus on the things that are important to you?

QUESTION 3: If you're a disciplined person who prefers order, calendaring time for each activity (also known as time blocking) is a good way to help create the balance you seek. If schedules and timelines feel rigid, consider planning a certain amount of time every day or week to pursue particular activities. Perhaps set aside one day of the week to get certain things done to avoid feeling hemmed in. Today, block off a meaningful amount of time next week to pursue your new goal. Balance that with time for other activities – family, friends, exercise, and leisure.

If we act as the CEO of our lives, we know how to direct our healing, drive our success, and implement strategies for our happiest outcomes.

TIP #38 – Reflect (Ongoing)

Reflection is a powerful tool for aligning your intentions, analyzing an issue, or resting from the daily grind of life. But it's not as easy as it sounds. At home and at work, technology intrudes on every facet of our lives. As technology continues to become a more essential part of our lives, we must be very careful to avoid succumbing entirely to its call. We must **make a point** to unplug and find some personal quiet time every day.

Doctors and employers preach that sitting for long periods of time in front of the computer is not healthy for us, but we often find ourselves unable to push away from the desk and take a break. We know we are headed in a dangerous direction, but our deadlines and inflexibility keep us from taking the necessary steps to maintain our health. We must be creative and find the time to stand, walk, or stretch for a few minutes every hour. If this seems impossible at work, then we need to be selfish at home and steal a few minutes here and there throughout the day for solitude.

You don't have to be in Yinchuan, China or Beloviste, Macedonia to find a quiet spot; you can certainly seek peace in your own backyard. Make every effort to disconnect from all sources of interference for at least 30 minutes daily to achieve clarity and focus.

QUESTION 1:   How much time do you presently take on a daily basis for prayer, reflection, meditation, or rejuvenation?

QUESTION 2: If this concept is foreign – or uncomfortable – for you, start small. Shut your office door – or better yet, go outside to a quiet spot – and set a timer for five minutes. Close your eyes and just focus on your breathing. Notice how your body feels. Notice the sounds around you. Breathe – in and out. Notice yourself relaxing and feel the stress leaving your body. Work up to doing this three or four times a day – eventually increasing the time to a half-hour at least once a day. Journal your experiences.

QUESTION 3: Once you've begun successfully spending even a

few moments of quiet every day, notice how your thinking changes. Are you more focused? More energized around your goal or passion? Do you have more energy for the people and activities in your life that matter most? Did you learn anything surprising once you committed to a daily reflection practice?

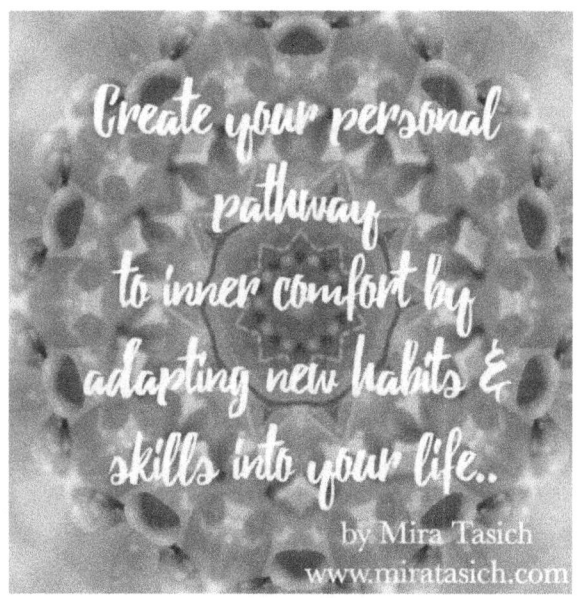

TIP #39 – Think "Proactively"

Thinking proactively means planning ahead, as opposed to waiting for something to happen and then reacting. A strategy is a plan of actions designed to achieve a goal. The keyword there is PLAN. Do you have a plan to achieve your goal – whether it's a new job, to start a business, to find the love of your life, or to make a cross-country move? To make such a plan, you've got to think proactively, which basically means thinking ahead and considering the factors that could affect your outcome. Who will you need on your team? What will you need to learn? What kinds of supplies will you need? What will it cost? How long should it take? Answers to all of these questions go into your action plan – your ultimate success strategy.

QUESTION 1: Identify the deficiencies between the resources you have and the ones you'll need to achieve your goal.

QUESTION 2: What additional tasks do you need to add to your daily routine to help you grow and expand your knowledge or expertise so that you can achieve your goal as quickly and easily as possible?

QUESTION 3: Step away from your plan for a few days or a week. Keep it in the back of your mind – but give your mind a chance to rest. Then review it again with new eyes. What might you have missed on the first go-round? Where are the gaps? Where can you tighten up aspects of the plan to make it more cohesive and efficient?

Do you have a plan to achieve your goal?

TIP #40 – Love Yourself, Always

Above all else, love yourself. Be humble. Listen to your own voice, be your own cheerleader, and recognize your instinct matters. Self-love isn't always easy, especially when we're at a crossroads or feeling disappointed with our circumstances. But that's when it's most crucial to speak well to yourself, rather than critically. Many of us are a product of being raised in a culture that teaches us to believe that to love ourselves is selfish. Do everything in your power to look your best and feel great physically (e.g., get enough sleep, exercise, drink lots of water). Use your affirmations to reinforce progress and good feelings.

At times when you are unsure what to do, weigh your options but don't overanalyze the situation. Go with your gut feeling. It is OK to consider other people's opinions if they offer a different perspective on your situation. **However, you are the most qualified person to align your needs and wants with your goals.** Be grateful for their advice, but use only what works for you. In fact, be grateful for all that you have. Keep in mind that the people who love you often may not be in a position to give you what you want or need. Be kind to them, regardless.

I was raised to think I must cater to everyone first before I consider doing things for myself. I had to work hard on changing my ways and still struggle at times. One thing I realized – when I became passionate about completing my writing projects, that turned out to be my priority. I learned to be more protective of my space and time in order to accomplish my goals.

QUESTION 1: When you look in the mirror, who do you see? Do you treat that person with kind thoughts and gentleness, or criticism and negative emotions?

QUESTION 2: What habits, behaviors, and mannerisms have you developed over the years to please others? They often don't help us, but we hold on to them because of their familiarity. You need habits, behaviors and mannerisms that align with your present state. How can you begin to release those habits and adopt new ones more suited to your own needs?

QUESTION 3: What new thoughts, actions, and traditions can you adopt so that you can start behaving as your own best friend? If these are not easy at first, step into them a little at a time. Try an affirmation like, "I'm ready to love myself more." Soon you'll be able to transition it to, "I love myself!" or "I like what I see in the mirror!"

LIFEHACKS: 40 Tips for Rewriting Your Life

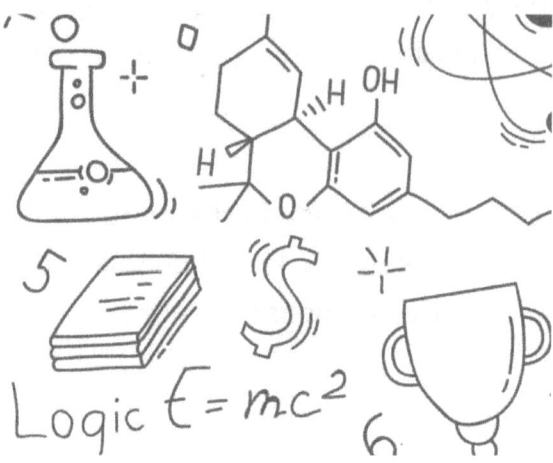

**Explore and celebrate your talents!
It is never too late to live a fulfilling life.**

Challenge yourself to pursue continuous growth and mind expansion. Not only is this important for self-renewal, but it will enhance your self-esteem, your self-confidence, and your personal innovation efforts.

Conclusion

Transformations do not always come quickly. Often, the transformative path is not clear, but rather a winding road over hills and through some valleys. Small signs can easily be misunderstood and missed if you are not careful. As I stated in my book, **Good Bye Job, Hello Life**: *"Finding a job linked to our passions and living a fuller, more meaningful life can be challenging. Our passions are not always identifiable. At times, patience, drive, persistence, and open mindedness help to uncover them".*

I write from my personal history. I faced many challenges including growing up as a poor child in an environment of limited means, being sent as teenager to a new country with a different language and culture to live with my estranged mother and new stepfather; finding a way to build a career while overcoming certain learned cultural barriers; overcoming an abusive relationship; losing a career that became part of my identity. I most definitely hit the bottom only to find my passion and rise again. I rejuvenated my life and discovered my mission after moving to Arizona for my new career and uncovered my creative talent as an author.

I hope this book inspires you to see your challenges as opportunities, not setbacks. Remember these aphorisms:

1. **You can overcome any obstacle. Obstacles may be opportunities in disguise. Changes may be difficult to face, but that is how we keep growing.**

2. **It is essential to keep rejuvenating your life. Self-renewal is important to our well-being and the key to thriving in any environment. Creativity and self-reflecting are just as important. Love and embrace your authentic self. You are unique and have an important purpose on this earth.**

3. **You already have the tools to find balance and embrace the important elements in your life. What it takes is keeping resilient, inspired, and determined to find, live, and sustain your best life.**

Your new dream may seem big and unreachable at this moment. Be persistent, make a plan, and continue to strive for it! Start by loving yourself first, living mindfully, listening to your authentic voice, and being grateful for what you already have. Take steps daily to keep your goal and passion alive. Be sure to free yourself from personal and cultural limitations. And through it all, be kind to others, respectful even to people from unfamiliar cultures or those with whom you disagree or people you don't understand.

Look back through your journal and examine your answers to the questions for Tips #1 through #40. How does your story read now?

LIFEHACKS: 40 Tips for Rewriting Your Life

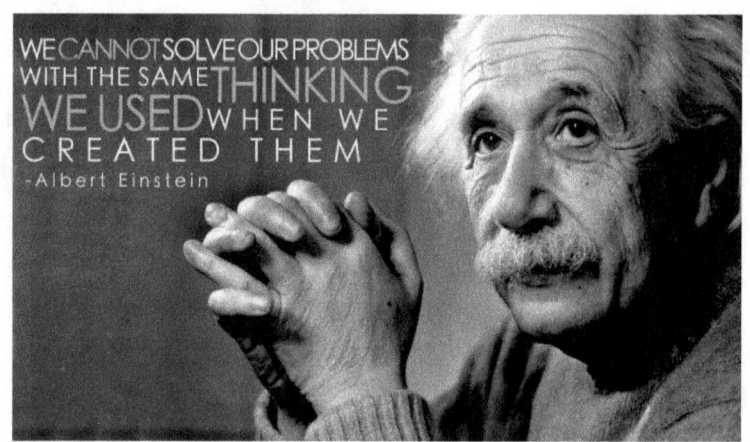

Planning & Progress Tracking

Tracking Your Progress

This is optional. However, in order to support and encourage your journey, it is beneficial to track your progress. The Segment Table at the bottom of the page is provided so that you can schedule your start dates when you are ready to begin to work on each segment. Form may be downloaded: www.miratasich.com

Segment	Resources Needed	Start Date	End Date	Comments
Dealing Directly with the Initial Impact				
Holistic Self-Care				
Rechanneling of Energies				
Life & Career Rejuvenation				
Stay in the CEO Lane of your Life				

Activity Sheet

If you don't have time to plan, we've created a guide to help you take actions immediately. Pick and choose what you like. Form may be downloaded: www.miratasich.com

Segment	Tip	Activity	Completion Date
Dealing Directly	Believe It; Don't Deny It		
Dealing Directly	Don't Panic! Remain Calm		
Dealing Directly	Deal With Sadness		
Dealing Directly	Deal With Anger		
Holistic Self-Care	Detox		
Holistic Self-Care	Massage Therapy		
Holistic Self-Care	Recuperate/Heal		
Holistic Self-Care	Commit to Hiatus/Take a Pause		
Holistic Self-Care	Explore Nature's Hot Springs		
Holistic Self-Care	Get a Makeover/Pamper Yourself		
Holistic Self-Care	Dance		
Holistic Self-Care	Spiritual Renewal		
Holistic Self-Care	Create Your Own Zen-like Space or Experience		
Holistic Self-Care	Music Therapy		
Re-Channeling En	Get to Know Yourself		
Re-Channeling En	Keep a Journal		
Re-Channeling En	Travel or Act as a Tourist in Your City		
Re-Channeling En	Find a Hobby		
Re-Channeling En	Expand Your World/Keep on Learning		
Re-Channeling En	Get your Creative On		
Re-Channeling En	Volunteer		
Re-Channeling En	Spread Kindness		
Re-Channeling En	Expand Your Vision		
Re-Channeling En	Passion Meets you		
Life & Career Rejuv	Redefine/Reinvent Your Purpose		
Life & Career Rejuv	Socialize/Network/Search for Support		
Life & Career Rejuv	Develop Your Plan of Action		
Life & Career Rejuv	Go into Action		
Life & Career Rejuv	Look the Part		

LIFEHACKS: 40 Tips for Rewriting Your Life

Segment	Tip	Activity	Completion Date
Stay in the CEO Lane of Your Life	Living with the "New Normal"		
Stay in the CEO Lane of Your Life	Stay Positive		
Stay in the CEO Lane of Your Life	Be Flexible		
Stay in the CEO Lane of Your Life	Create Your Own Uplift Drill		
Stay in the CEO Lane of Your Life	Build Your Insp Boost File		
Stay in the CEO Lane of Your Life	Embrace Diversity (Yours and Others')		
Stay in the CEO Lane of Your Life	Retool Your Attitude Continuously		
Stay in the CEO Lane of Your Life	Realign Your Actions to Balance		
Stay in the CEO Lane of Your Life	Reflect (Ongoing)		
Stay in the CEO Lane of Your Life	Think "Proactively"		
Stay in the CEO Lane of Your Life	Love Yourself, Always		

ABOUT THE AUTHOR

As a young teenager, Mira Tasich moved to the United States from Eastern Europe (the former Yugoslavia). After mastering English, she successfully navigated a new culture and achieved financial and professional success as an entrepreneur and as a corporate employee. Her skills at financial analysis, project management, business planning, and technical support in the aerospace, automotive, and retail, industries allowed her to realize an immigrant's goal - the American Dream.

However, her belief in her happiness and her definition of success were shaken after her job in the automotive industry was eliminated and she felt stripped of her identity and self esteem. Embarking on a journey of discovery, Mira reassessed her motivations and life goals and reconciled her cultural, family, and creative influences. She discovered her talents as a painter, photographer, jewelry designer, and writer while also slowing the pace of her life and seeking and finding solace in nature and other Zen-like spaces.

In her award winning book, **Good Bye Job, Hello Life**, Mira shares her insights with her readers as she moves from disillusionment, to confusion, and finally to reconciliation and happiness. Her readers and fans made her realize she possesses the ability to keep rejuvenating her life. With their encouragement, she decided to help others reassess and turn around their lives. And, the result is her workbook, **LIFEHACKS: 40 Tips for Rewriting Your Life.** She continues to work on her own journey, to connect with people of all cultures and to inspire others to live happier lives.

Mira lives in Phoenix, Arizona, with her husband and continues to value and enjoy her creative talents.

Miratasich.com
Creativedreammedia.com

www.ingramcontent.com/pod-product-compliance
Lightning Source LLC
Chambersburg PA
CBHW061651040426
42446CB00010B/1688